LEARNING SANSKRIT FOR SCHOOL STUDENTS

DR DHEERAJ MEHROTRA

Contents

PREFACE

This book, Learning Sanskrit for School Students, is designed to make your journey into this ancient language enjoyable and rewarding. Learning a new language can seem daunting, exceptionally as structured and nuanced as Sanskrit. That's why we've created a step-by-step guide that breaks down the complexities into manageable and engaging lessons. Whether you are a beginner or looking to strengthen your existing skills, this book will provide the tools you need to succeed.

This book is structured to guide you through the fundamentals of Sanskrit logically and progressively. Start with the basics, such as the Sanskrit alphabet and simple words, and gradually move on to forming sentences and understanding grammar. Practice regularly, and don't hesitate to revisit previous lessons to reinforce your understanding. Most importantly, enjoy the process of learning and discovering the beauty of Sanskrit.

I hope this book inspires you to explore the depths of Sanskrit and appreciate its timeless beauty. May your journey be filled with curiosity, joy, and a deep sense of accomplishment.

शुभमस्तु!
(May it be auspicious!)

— The Author

I
The Alphabets

The Alphabets of Sanskrit

Sanskrit is one of the oldest languages in the world. It boasts a rich and intricate system of writing that has influenced many modern languages. This chapter will discuss Sanskrit's alphabets, detailing their structure, pronunciation, and significance in linguistic history and cultural heritage.

Overview of Sanskrit Alphabets

Sanskrit is primarily written in two scripts: Devanagari and Romanized Sanskrit. The Devanagari script is the most widely used and consists of 47 primary characters, including 14 vowels and 33 consonants. Each character has a unique sound and is integral to the phonetic nature of the language.

Vowels

The vowels in Sanskrit are categorized into short and long sounds. Here is a list of the vowels:

Short Vowels:

अ *(a)*

इ *(i)*

उ *(u)*

ऋ *(ṛ)*

ऌ (*ḷ*)

Long Vowels:

आ (*ā*)

ई (*ī*)

ऊ (*ū*)

ॠ (*ṝ*)

ॡ (*ḹ*)

Consonants

Sanskrit consonants are classified based on their articulation. They can be grouped into several categories:

Gutturals: क *(ka),* ख *(kha),* ग *(ga),* घ *(gha),* ङ *(ṅa)*

Palatals: च *(cha),* छ *(chha),* ज *(ja),* झ *(jha),* ञ *(ña)*

Cerebrals: ट *(ṭa),* ठ *(ṭha),* ड *(ḍa),* ढ *(ḍha),* ण *(ṇa)*

Dentals: त *(ta),* थ *(tha),* द *(da),* ध *(dha),* न *(na)*

Labials: प *(pa),* फ *(pha),* ब *(ba),* भ *(bha),* म *(ma)*

Semi-vowels: य *(ya),* र *(ra),* ल *(la),* व *(va)*

Sibilants: श *(śa),* ष *(ṣa),* स *(sa)*

Glottal: ह *(ha)*

Vowels (स्वर - Svara)

अआइईउऊऋॠऌएऐओऔ

aāiīuūṛṝḷeaioau

Consonants (व्यंजन - Vyanjana)

Gutturals (कण्ठ्य - *Kaṇṭhya*)

कखगघङ

kakhagaghaṅa

Palatals (तालव्य - *Tālavya*)

चछजझञ

cachajajhaña

Cerebrals (मूर्धन्य - *Mūrdhanya*)

टठडढण

ṭaṭhaḍaḍhaṇa

Dentals (दन्त्य - *Dantya*)

तथदधन

tathadadhana

Labials (ओष्ठ्य - Oṣṭhya)

पफबभम

paphababhama

Semi-Vowels (अन्तःस्थ - Antaḥstha)

यरलव

yaralava

Sibilants (उष्म - Uṣma)

शषसह

śaṣasaha

Additional Sounds

Anusvāra (अं) → ṁ (nasalization)

Visarga (अः) → ḥ (breath-like sound)

Importance of Sanskrit Alphabets

The Sanskrit alphabets are not just a means of communication; they reflect the culture and philosophy of ancient India. Sanskrit's precise phonetics allows for a rich expression of ideas and emotions, making it a preferred language for spiritual texts, poetry, and classical literature.

Understanding the Sanskrit alphabet is essential for anyone interested in the language's literature, philosophy, and cultural significance. The intricate system of vowels and consonants facilitates communication and preserves the profound wisdom embedded in ancient texts. As we delve deeper into the study of Sanskrit, we uncover the beauty and complexity of one of humanity's oldest languages.

Multiple Type Questions

1. How many primary characters does the Sanskrit Devanagari script have?
   A) 36
B) 44
C) 47
D) 50
   Answer: C) 47
   2. Which of the following is NOT a short vowel in Sanskrit?
   A) अ (a)
B) इ (i)
C) उ (u)

D) ई (ī)

Answer: D) ई (ī)

3. How many long vowels are there in Sanskrit?

A) 5

B) 6

C) 7

D) 8

Answer: B) 6

4. Which category does the letter 'ट' (ṭa) belong to?

A) Guttural

B) Palatal

C) Cerebral

D) Dental

Answer: C) Cerebral

5. Which of the following is a labial consonant?

A) प (pa)

B) त (ta)

C) च (cha)

D) ह (ha)

Answer: A) प (pa)

6. What is the phonetic term for 'Semi-Vowels' in Sanskrit?

A) उष्म (Uṣma)

B) अन्तःस्थ (Antaḥstha)

C) दन्त्य (Dantya)

D) मूर्धन्य (Mūrdhanya)

Answer: B) अन्तःस्थ (Antaḥstha)

7. Which of these is a sibilant consonant?

A) न (na)

B) भ (bha)

C) श (śa)

D) व (va)

Answer: C) श (śa)

8. What is the term for nasalization in Sanskrit?

A) Visarga

B) Anusvāra

C) Antaḥstha

D) Dantya

Answer: B) Anusvāra

9. How many vowels are there in Sanskrit?

A) 10

B) 12

C) 14

D) 16

Answer: C) 14

10. Which of these is NOT a guttural consonant?

A) क (ka)

B) ग (ga)

C) घ (gha)

D) च (cha)

Answer: D) च (cha)

11. The letter 'ञ' (ña) belongs to which category?

A) Guttural

B) Palatal

C) Labial

D) Cerebral

Answer: B) Palatal

12. What is the Romanized representation of ऋ?

A) ri

B) ṛ

C) ru

D) r

Answer: B) ṛ

13. The consonant 'म' (ma) belongs to which category?

A) Labial

B) Dental

C) Cerebral

D) Palatal

Answer: A) Labial

14. Which of the following is a breath-like sound in Sanskrit?

A) अ॑ (ṁ)

B) अः (ḥ)

C) ङ (ṅ)

D) ष (ṣ)

Answer: B) अः (ḥ)

15. The letter 'व' (va) is classified as?

A) Semi-vowel

B) Sibilant

C) Dental

D) Cerebral

Answer: A) Semi-vowel

16. The letter 'र' (ra) is a part of which group?

A) Uṣma

B) Antaḥstha

C) Dantya

D) Mūrdhanya

Answer: B) Antaḥstha

17. Which of the following is NOT a long vowel?

A) आ (ā)

B) ई (ī)

C) ऊ (ū)

D) इ (i)

Answer: D) इ (i)

18. How many guttural consonants are there in Sanskrit?

A) 4

B) 5

C) 6

D) 7

Answer: B) 5

19. What is the correct sequence of dental consonants?

A) त, थ, द, ध, न

B) क, ख, ग, घ, ङ

C) च, छ, ज, झ, ञ

D) ट, ठ, ड, ढ, ण

Answer: A) त, थ, द, ध, न

20. Which is the correct representation of the consonants in the Palatal group?

A) ट, ठ, ड, ढ, ण

B) क, ख, ग, घ, ङ

C) च, छ, ज, झ, ञ

D) प, फ, ब, भ, म

Answer: C) च, छ, ज, झ, ञ

21. The letter 'ष' (ṣa) belongs to which category?

A) Cerebral

B) Sibilant

C) Labial

D) Semi-Vowel

Answer: B) Sibilant

22. Which script is commonly used to write Sanskrit?

A) Arabic

B) Devanagari

C) Cyrillic

D) Latin

Answer: B) Devanagari

23. Which of these is NOT an official vowel in Sanskrit?

A) ए (e)

B) ऐ (ai)

C) अः (ḥ)

D) औ (au)

Answer: C) अः (ḥ)

24. The letter 'ह' (ha) belongs to which category?

A) Semi-vowel

B) Glottal

C) Sibilant

D) Palatal

   Answer: B) Glottal

   25. What is the significance of Sanskrit alphabets?

   A) They help in daily communication only

B) They are mainly used in modern European languages

C) They preserve the phonetic structure of the language and carry cultural heritage

D) They are no longer in use

   Answer: C) They preserve the phonetic structure of the language and carry cultural heritage

II
Numbers in Sanskrit

Sanskrit Numbers (संस्कृत संख्याः)

Number/ Devanagari/ Transliteration

1 १ एक (eka)

2 २ द्वि (*dvi*)

3 ३ त्रि (*tri*)

4 ४ चतुः- (*chatur*)

5 ५ पञ्च (*pañca*)

6 ६ षट् (*ṣaṭ*)

7 ७ सप्त (*sapta*)

8 ८ अष्ट (*aṣṭa*)

9 ९ नव (*nava*)

10 १० दश (*daśa*)

11 ११ एकादश (*ekādaśa*)

12 १२ द्वादश (*dvādaśa*)

13 १३ त्रयोदश (*trayodaśa*)

14 १४ चतुर्दश (*chaturdaśa*)

15 १५ पञ्चदश (*pañcadaśa*)

16 १६ षोडश (*ṣoḍaśa*)

17 १७ सप्तदश (*saptadaśa*)

18 १८ अष्टादश (*aṣṭādaśa*)

19 १९ एकोनवशिंति (*ekonaviṁśati*)

20 २० वशिंति (*viṁśati*)

21 to 30

21 - एकवशिंति (*Ekaviṁśati*)

22 - द्वाविंशति (*Dvāviṃśati*)

23 - त्रयोविंशति (*Trayoviṃśati*)

24 - चतुर्विंशति (*Caturviṃśati*)

25 - पञ्चविंशति (*Pañcaviṃśati*)

26 - षड्विंशति (*Ṣaḍviṃśati*)

27 - सप्तविंशति (*Saptaviṃśati*)

28 - अष्टाविंशति (*Aṣṭāviṃśati*)

29 - नवविंशति (*Navaviṃśati*)

30 - त्रिंशत् (*Trimśat*)

31 to 40

31 - एकत्रिंशत् (*Ekatriṃśat*)

32 - द्वात्रिंशत् (*Dvâtriṃśat*)

33 - त्रयस्त्रिंशत् (*Trayastriṃśat*)

34 - चतुस्त्रिंशत् (*Caturtriṃśat*)

35 - पञ्चत्रिंशत् (*Pañcatriṃśat*)

36 - षट्त्रिंशत् (*Ṣaṭtriṃśat*)

37 - सप्तत्रिंशत् (*Saptatriṃśat*)

38 - अष्टात्रिंशत् (*Aṣṭātriṃśat*)

39 - नवत्रिंशत् (*Navatriṃśat*)

40 - चत्वारिंशत् (*Catvāriṃśat*)

Forming Larger Numbers

Sanskrit combines the words for the base numbers to form more significant numbers. For example:

21 is expressed as "वशितिः एकम्" (viṃśati ekam).

35 is expressed as "त्रशित् पञ्च" (trimśat pañca).

1000 is "सहस्रम्" (sahasram).

Understanding numbers in Sanskrit is essential for anyone interested in the language, mathematics, or ancient Indian culture. The systematic way numbers are formed and combined reflects the sophistication of Sanskrit as a language and its mathematical heritage.

Multiple Type Questions

1. What is the Sanskrit word for the number 1?

    A) द्वि (dvi)

B) एक (eka)

C) त्रि (tri)

D) चतुः (chatur)

    Answer: B) एक (eka)

    2. How is the number 10 written in Sanskrit?

    A) दश (daśa)

B) नव (nava)

C) अष्ट (aṣṭa)

D) एकादश (ekādaśa)

    Answer: A) दश (daśa)

    3. What is the Sanskrit transliteration of 8?

    A) सप्त (sapta)

B) अष्ट (aṣṭa)

C) नव (nava)

D) षट् (ṣaṭ)

    Answer: B) अष्ट (aṣṭa)

    4. Which of these is the Sanskrit number for 15?

    A) षड्वशिंति (Ṣaḍviṃśati)

B) त्रयोदश (trayodaśa)

C) पञ्चदश (pañcadaśa)

D) सप्तदश (saptadaśa)

    Answer: C) पञ्चदश (pañcadaśa)

    5. How do you say 20 in Sanskrit?

    A) नवत्रशित् (Navatriṃśat)

B) दश (daśa)

C) वशिंति (viṃśati)

D) चतुर्दश (chaturdaśa)

    Answer: C) वशिंति (viṃśati)

    6. What is the correct Sanskrit word for 7?

    A) नव (nava)

B) सप्त (sapta)

C) अष्ट (aṣṭa)

D) पञ्च (pañca)

    Answer: B) सप्त (sapta)

    7. Which of these is 24 in Sanskrit?

    A) त्रयोदश (trayodaśa)

B) चतुर्वशिंति (Caturviṃśati)

C) पञ्चत्रशित् (Pañcatriṃśat)

D) सप्तदश (saptadaśa)

Answer: B) चतुर्वशिंति (Caturviṃśati)

8. What is the Sanskrit term for 1000?

A) शत (śata)

B) सहस्रम् (sahasram)

C) चत्वारशित् (Catvāriṃśat)

D) त्रशित् (Triṃśat)

Answer: B) सहस्रम् (sahasram)

9. How do you say 39 in Sanskrit?

A) नवत्रशित् (Navatriṃśat)

B) षट्त्रशित् (Ṣaṭtriṃśat)

C) सप्तत्रशित् (Saptatriṃśat)

D) त्रशित् (Triṃśat)

Answer: A) नवत्रशित् (Navatriṃśat)

10. What is the number 100 called in Sanskrit?

A) दश (daśa)

B) शत (śata)

C) त्रशित् (Triṃśat)

D) सहस्रम् (sahasram)

Answer: B) शत (śata)

11. What is 3 in Sanskrit?

A) त्रि (tri)

B) षट् (ṣaṭ)

C) सप्त (sapta)

D) द्वि (dvi)

Answer: A) त्रि (tri)

12. How is 50 written in Sanskrit?

A) षष्टि (ṣaṣṭi)

B) पञ्चाशत् (pañcāśat)

C) सप्तदश (saptadaśa)

D) त्रयोदश (trayodaśa)

Answer: B) पञ्चाशत् (pañcāśat)

13. What is 16 in Sanskrit?

A) षोडश (ṣoḍaśa)

B) षट् (ṣaṭ)

C) सप्त (sapta)

D) नव (nava)

Answer: A) षोडश (ṣoḍaśa)

14. Which Sanskrit number represents 31?

A) एकत्रशित् (Ekatriṃśat)

B) त्रयोदश (trayodaśa)

C) त्रशित् (Triṃśat)

D) सप्तदश (saptadaśa)

Answer: A) एकत्रशित् (Ekatriṃśat)

15. How is 19 written in Sanskrit?

A) त्रयोदश (trayodaśa)

B) सप्तत्रशित् (Saptatriṃśat)

C) नवत्रशित् (Navatriṃśat)

D) एकोनवशिति (ekonaviṃśati)

Answer: D) एकोनवशिति (ekonaviṃśati)

16. Which Sanskrit word represents the number 26?

A) षड्वशिति (Ṣaḍviṃśati)

B) पञ्चत्रशित् (Pañcatriṃśat)

C) सप्तत्रशित् (Saptatriṃśat)

D) अष्टात्रशित् (Aṣṭātriṃśat)

Answer: A) षड्वशिति (Ṣaḍviṃśati)

17. What is the Sanskrit term for 40?

A) चतुर्दश (chaturdaśa)

B) चत्वारशित् (Catvāriṃśat)

C) त्रयोदश (trayodaśa)

D) एकादश (ekādaśa)

Answer: B) चत्वारशित् (Catvāriṃśat)

18. How do you say 13 in Sanskrit?

A) त्रयोदश (trayodaśa)

B) पञ्चत्रंशित् (Pañcatrimśat)

C) चतुर्दश (chaturdaśa)

D) नवत्रंशित् (Navatrimśat)

Answer: A) त्रयोदश (trayodaśa)

19. What is 23 in Sanskrit?

A) त्रयोविंशिति (Trayovimśati)

B) त्रयोदश (trayodaśa)

C) नवत्रंशित् (Navatrimśat)

D) सप्तदश (saptadaśa)

Answer: A) त्रयोविंशिति (Trayovimśati)

20. What is the Sanskrit numeral for 17?

A) सप्तदश (saptadaśa)

B) पञ्चदश (pañcadaśa)

C) षड्विंशिति (Ṣaḍvimśati)

D) नवत्रंशित् (Navatrimśat)

Answer: A) सप्तदश (saptadaśa)

21. What is the Sanskrit term for 5?

A) षट् (ṣaṭ)

B) पञ्च (pañca)

C) सप्त (sapta)

D) नव (nava)

Answer: B) पञ्च (pañca)

22. How do you say 34 in Sanskrit?

A) त्रयोविंशिति (Trayovimśati)

B) चतुस्त्रंशित् (Caturtrimśat)

C) नवत्रंशित् (Navatrimśat)

D) त्रयोदश (Trayodaśa)

Answer: B) चतुस्त्रंशित् (Caturtrimśat)

23. Which of these is the correct Sanskrit number for 28?

A) अष्टावंशिति (Aṣṭāvimṣati)

B) एकत्रंशित् (Ekatrimṣat)

C) त्रंशित् (Trimṣat)

D) नवत्रंशित् (Navatrimṣat)

Answer: A) अष्टावंशिति (Aṣṭāvimṣati)

24. What is the Sanskrit word for 11?

A) एकादश (Ekādaśa)

B) द्वादश (Dvādaśa)

C) त्रयोदश (Trayodaśa)

D) सप्तदश (Saptadaśa)

Answer: A) एकादश (Ekādaśa)

25. What is the Sanskrit representation of 29?

A) नवत्रंशित् (Navatrimṣat)

B) नववंशिति (Navavimṣati)

C) सप्तत्रंशित् (Saptatrimṣat)

D) एकोनवंशिति (Ekonavimṣati)

Answer: B) नववंशिति (Navavimṣati)

III

Basic Vocabulary

1. Pronouns (सर्वनामानि)

अहम् (Aham) – I

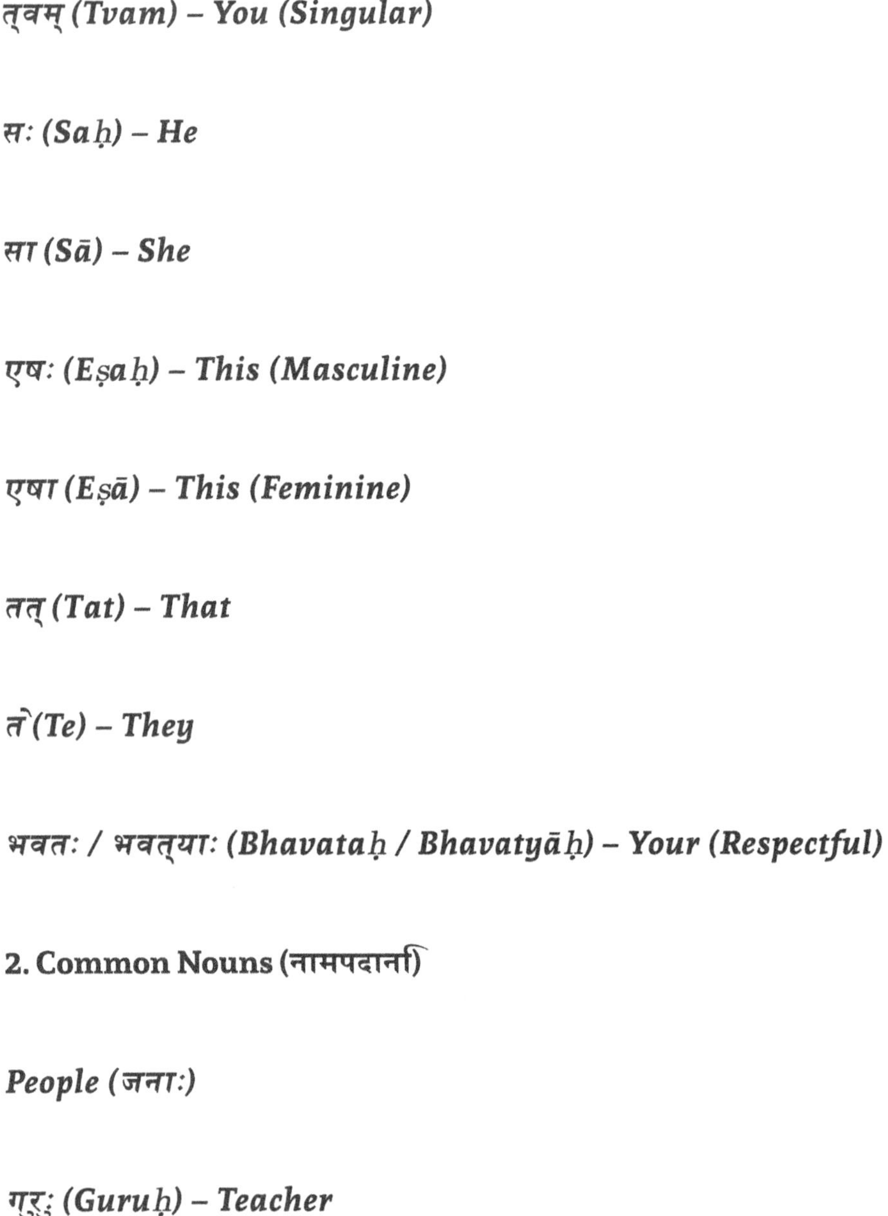

त्वम् (*Tvam*) – *You (Singular)*

स: (*Saḥ*) – *He*

सा (*Sā*) – *She*

एष: (*Eṣaḥ*) – *This (Masculine)*

एषा (*Eṣā*) – *This (Feminine)*

तत् (*Tat*) – *That*

ते (*Te*) – *They*

भवत: / भवत्या: (*Bhavataḥ / Bhavatyāḥ*) – *Your (Respectful)*

2. Common Nouns (नामपदानि)

People (जना:)

गुरु: (*Guruḥ*) – *Teacher*

शष्यिः *(Śiṣyaḥ)* – Student

पत्ति *(Pitā)* – Father

माता *(Mātā)* – Mother

भ्राता *(Bhrātā)* – Brother

भगिनी *(Bhaginī)* – Sister

मत्रिम् *(Mitram)* – Friend

राजा *(Rājā)* – King

रानी *(Rānī)* – Queen

Places (स्थानानि)

गृहम् *(Gṛham)* – House

वद्यिालयः *(Vidyālayaḥ)* – School

मन्दिरम् (*Mandiram*) – *Temple*

वनम् (*Vanam*) – *Forest*

नगरम् (*Nagaram*) – *City*

Things (वस्तूनि)

पुस्तकम् (*Pustakam*) – *Book*

फलम् (*Phalam*) – *Fruit*

पुष्पम् (*Puṣpam*) – *Flower*

जलम् (*Jalam*) – *Water*

मष्टिटान्नम् (*Miṣṭānnam*) – *Sweets*

3. Verbs (क्रियापदानि)

गच्छति (*Gacchati*) – *Goes*

आगच्छति *(Āgacchati)* – *Comes*

पठति *(Paṭhati)* – *Reads*

लेखति *(Lekhati)* – *Writes*

खादति *(Khādati)* – *Eats*

पिबति *(Pibati)* – *Drinks*

वदति *(Vadati)* – *Speaks*

श्रृणोति *(Śṛṇoti)* – *Hears*

गायति *(Gāyati)* – *Sings*

नृत्यति *(Nṛtyati)* – *Dances*

शोचति *(Śocati)* – *Thinks*

सुखम् *(Sukham)* – *Happy*

दुःखम् *(Duḥkham)* – *Sad*

लघु *(Laghu)* – *Light*

गुरु *(Guru)* – *Heavy*

शुभम् *(Śubham)* – *Good*

अशुभम् *(Aśubham)* – *Bad*

नवम् *(Navam)* – *New*

पुरातनम् *(Purātanam)* – *Old*

महान् *(Mahān)* – *Great*

4. Numbers (संख्याः)

एकम् *(Ekam)* – *One*

द्वे *(Dve)* – *Two*

त्रीणि *(Trīṇi) – Three*

चत्वारि *(Catvāri) – Four*

पञ्च *(Pañca) – Five*

षट् *(Ṣaṭ) – Six*

सप्त *(Sapta) – Seven*

अष्ट *(Aṣṭa) – Eight*

नव *(Nava) – Nine*

दश *(Daśa) – Ten*

5. Days of the Week (वारा:)

रविवासर: *(Ravivāsaraḥ) – Sunday*

सोमवासर: *(Somavāsaraḥ) – Monday*

मङ्गलवासर: *(Maṅgalavāsaraḥ)* – **Tuesday**

बुधवासर: *(Budhavāsaraḥ)* – **Wednesday**

गुरुवासर: *(Guruvāsaraḥ)* – **Thursday**

शुक्रवासर: *(Śukravāsaraḥ)* – **Friday**

शनिवासर: *(Śanivāsaraḥ)* – **Saturday**

6. Time Words (कालसंबन्धा:)

सर्वदा *(Sarvadā)* – **Always**

कदा? *(Kadā?)* – **When?**

अद्य *(Adya)* – **Today**

श्व: *(Śvaḥ)* – **Tomorrow**

ह्य: *(Hyaḥ)* – **Yesterday**

पूरातः *(Prātaḥ) – Morning*

साय *(Sāyaṁ) – Evening*

रात्रौ *(Rātrau) – At night*

7. Prepositions (उपसर्गाः)

मध्ये *(Madhye) – In between*

अग्रे *(Agre) – In front*

पश्चात् *(Paścāt) – Behind*

सह *(Saha) – With*

वनिा *(Vinā) – Without*

8. Family Members (कुटुम्बसंबन्धाः)

पिता *(Pitā) – Father*

माता *(Mātā)* – **Mother**

भ्राता *(Bhrātā)* – **Brother**

भगिनी *(Bhaginī)* – **Sister**

पुत्रः *(Putraḥ)* – **Son**

पुत्री *(Putrī)* – **Daughter**

मातामहः *(Mātāmahaḥ)* – *Grandfather (Maternal)*

मातामही *(Mātāmahī)* – *Grandmother (Maternal)*

पितामहः *(Pitāmahaḥ)* – *Grandfather (Paternal)*

पितामही *(Pitāmahī)* – *Grandmother (Paternal)*

9. Greetings and Common Expressions (नमस्काराः च सामान्यवाक्यानि)

नमस्ते *(Namaste)* – **Hello**

हरिः ॐ (*Hariḥ Om*) – *Greetings in a spiritual context*

कथमस्ति भवान् / भवती? (*Kathamasti Bhavān / Bhavatī?*) – *How are you?*

अहं कुशली अस्मि (*Ahaṁ Kuśalī Asmi*) – *I am fine*

धन्यवादः (*Dhanyavādaḥ*) – *Thank you*

क्षम्यताम् (*Kṣamyatām*) – *Sorry / Excuse me*

शुभमस्तु (*Śubhamastu*) – *May it be auspicious*

पुनर्मिलामः (*Punarmilāmaḥ*) – *See you again*

सर्वं कुशलम्? (*Sarvaṁ Kuśalam?*) – *Is everything fine?*

सर्वं कुशलम्! (*Sarvaṁ Kuśalam!*) – *Everything is fine*

This is a comprehensive beginner's Sanskrit vocabulary list that can be a great starting point for learning the language.

Multiple Type Questions

1. What is the Sanskrit word for "I"?

A) त्वम् (Tvam)

B) स: (Saḥ)

C) अहम् (Aham)

D) ते (Te)

Answer: C) अहम् (Aham)

2. What is the correct Sanskrit term for "Teacher"?

A) शिष्य: (Śiṣyaḥ)

B) पिता (Pitā)

C) गुरु: (Guruḥ)

D) माता (Mātā)

Answer: C) गुरु: (Guruḥ)

3. How do you say "House" in Sanskrit?

A) विद्यालय: (Vidyālayaḥ)

B) मन्दिरम् (Mandiram)

C) गृहम् (Gṛham)

D) नगरम् (Nagaram)

Answer: C) गृहम् (Gṛham)

4. What is the Sanskrit term for "Fruit"?

A) पुष्पम् (Puṣpam)

B) जलम् (Jalam)

C) फलम् (Phalam)

D) पुस्तकं (Pustakam)

Answer: C) फलम् (Phalam)

5. Which of the following means "Reads" in Sanskrit?

A) लिखति (Lekhati)

B) पठति (Paṭhati)

C) गच्छति (Gacchati)

D) वदति (Vadati)

Answer: B) पठति (Paṭhati)

6. What is the Sanskrit number for "Five"?

A) चत्वारि (Catvāri)

B) षट् (Ṣaṭ)

C) सप्त (Sapta)

D) पञ्च (Pañca)

Answer: D) पञ्च (Pañca)

7. What is the Sanskrit term for "Sunday"?

A) सोमवासर: (Somavāsaraḥ)

B) बुधवासर: (Budhavāsaraḥ)

C) रविवासर: (Ravivāsaraḥ)

D) शनिवासर: (Śanivāsaraḥ)

Answer: C) रविवासर: (Ravivāsaraḥ)

8. How do you say "Tomorrow" in Sanskrit?

A) अद्य (Adya)

B) श्व: (Śvaḥ)

C) ह्य: (Hyaḥ)

D) कदा (Kadā)

Answer: B) श्व: (Śvaḥ)

9. What does "विना" (Vinā) mean?

A) In front

B) Behind

C) With

D) Without

Answer: D) Without

10. Which word represents "Daughter" in Sanskrit?

A) भ्राता (Bhrātā)

B) पुत्र: (Putraḥ)

C) पुत्री (Putrī)

D) माता (Mātā)

Answer: C) पुत्री (Putrī)

11. What is the Sanskrit word for "Queen"?

A) रानी (Rānī)

B) राजा (Rājā)

C) माता (Mātā)

D) भगिनी (Bhaginī)

    Answer: A) रानी (Rānī)

    12. How do you say "Flower" in Sanskrit?

    A) पुस्तकं (Pustakam)

B) पुष्पम् (Puṣpam)

C) जलम् (Jalam)

D) मष्टिटान्नम् (Miṣṭānnam)

    Answer: B) पुष्पम् (Puṣpam)

    13. Which word means "Eats" in Sanskrit?

    A) गच्छति (Gacchati)

B) पठति (Paṭhati)

C) खादति (Khādati)

D) वदति (Vadati)

    Answer: C) खादति (Khādati)

    14. What is the Sanskrit word for "Three"?

    A) एकम् (Ekam)

B) द्वे (Dve)

C) त्रीणि (Trīṇi)

D) दश (Daśa)

    Answer: C) त्रीणि (Trīṇi)

    15. What does "धन्यवादः" (Dhanyavādaḥ) mean?

    A) Sorry

B) Thank you

C) See you again

D) Good

    Answer: B) Thank you

    16. Which of the following means "Morning" in Sanskrit?

    A) प्रातः (Prātaḥ)

B) सायं (Sāyaṁ)

C) रात्रौ (Rātrau)

D) ह्यः (Hyaḥ)

Answer: A) प्रातः (Prātaḥ)

17. What is the Sanskrit word for "Behind"?
A) पश्चात् (Paścāt)

B) अग्रे (Agre)

C) मध्ये (Madhye)

D) सह (Saha)

Answer: A) पश्चात् (Paścāt)

18. How do you say "Brother" in Sanskrit?
A) भगिनी (Bhaginī)

B) भ्राता (Bhrātā)

C) पिता (Pitā)

D) माता (Mātā)

Answer: B) भ्राता (Bhrātā)

19. What is the Sanskrit word for "Book"?
A) पुस्तकं (Pustakam)

B) फलम् (Phalam)

C) जलम् (Jalam)

D) पुष्पम् (Puṣpam)

Answer: A) पुस्तकं (Pustakam)

20. How do you say "Friend" in Sanskrit?
A) मित्रम् (Mitram)

B) राजा (Rājā)

C) शष्यिः (Śiṣyaḥ)

D) गुरुः (Guruḥ)

Answer: A) मित्रम् (Mitram)

21. What does "अशुभम्" (Aśubham) mean?
A) Good

B) Heavy

C) Bad

D) Happy

Answer: C) Bad

22. What is the Sanskrit word for "New"?

A) गुरु (Guru)

B) नवम् (Navam)

C) पुरातनम् (Purātanam)

D) महन् (Mahān)

Answer: B) नवम् (Navam)

23. Which of the following means "Dances" in Sanskrit?

A) गायति (Gāyati)

B) नृत्यति (Nṛtyati)

C) वदति (Vadati)

D) शोचति (Śocati)

Answer: B) नृत्यति (Nṛtyati)

24. What is the Sanskrit term for "Good"?

A) अशुभम् (Aśubham)

B) शुभम् (Śubham)

C) दुःखम् (Duḥkham)

D) सुखम् (Sukham)

Answer: B) शुभम् (Śubham)

25. How do you say "See you again" in Sanskrit?

A) पुनर्मिलामः (Punarmilāmaḥ)

B) हरिः ॐ (Hariḥ Om)

C) कथमस्ति भवान्? (Kathamasti Bhavān?)

D) नमस्ते (Namaste)

Answer: A) पुनर्मिलामः (Punarmilāmaḥ)

౮

IV
Everyday Conversations

1. Greetings and Introductions

नमस्ते

Namaste.

Hello.

൞

भवतः नाम किम्?

Bhavataḥ nāma kim?

What is your name? (formal)

൞

मम नाम रामः।

Mama nāma Rāmaḥ.

My name is Rama.

ॐ

भवान् कुत्र वसति?

Bhavān kutra vasati?

Where do you live? (formal)

ॐ

अहं दल्लीनगरे वसामि।

Ahaṃ Dillīnagare vasāmi.

I live in Delhi.

ॐ

2. At School

अद्य कः दविसः?

Adya kaḥ divasaḥ?

What day is today?

౪

अद्य सोमवासरः।

Adya Somavāsaraḥ.

Today is Monday.

౪

भवतः पाठः समाप्तः कम्?

Bhavataḥ pāṭhaḥ samāptaḥ kim?

Have you finished your lesson?

౪

न, अद्य अहं गृहकार्यं करोमि।

Na, adya aham gṛhakāryam karomi.

No, today I am doing homework.

৪৩

शिक्षकः कुत्र अस्ति?

Śikṣakaḥ kutra asti?

Where is the teacher?

৪৩

3. At Home

मातः, अहं क्षुधार्तः अस्मि।

Mātaḥ, aham kṣudhārtaḥ asmi.

Mother, I am hungry.

౪

पतिः, कदा वयं भ्रमणं गच्छामः?

Pitaḥ, kadā vayaṃ bhramaṇaṃ gacchāmaḥ?

Father, when are we going for a walk?

౪

भ्रातः, त्वं किं किरोषि?

Bhrātaḥ, tvaṃ kiṃ karosi?

Brother, what are you doing?

౪

अहं पुस्तकं पठामि।

Aham pustakam paṭhāmi.

I am reading a book.

౪

गृहे कः आगच्छति?

Gṛhe kaḥ āgacchati?

Who is coming home?

౪

4. Shopping

इदं कियत् मूल्यम् अस्ति?

Idaṃ kiyat mūlyam asti?

How much does this cost?

౪

इदं पञ्चाशत् रूप्यकाणि।

Idaṃ pañcāśat rūpyakāṇi.

This is fifty rupees.

৪০

भवती किं विक्रेतुम् इच्छति?

Bhavatī kiṃ viketum icchati?

What would you like to sell?

৪০

अहं फलानि क्रेतुम् इच्छामि।

Ahaṃ phalāni kretum icchāmi.

I want to buy fruits.

৪০

कृपया एतत् पैकेटं ददातु।

Kṛpayā etat paikeṭaṃ dadātu.

Please give me this packet.

೮

5. Dining Out

अत्र कः व्यञ्जनः श्रेष्ठः अस्ति?

Atra kaḥ vyañjanaḥ śreṣṭhaḥ asti?

What is the best dish here?

೮

मम पाकः अतीव स्वादष्टिः अस्ति।

Mama pākaḥ atīva svādiṣṭaḥ asti.

My food is very delicious.

☙

अहं जलं पातुम् इच्छामि

Ahaṃ jalaṃ pātum icchāmi.

I want to drink water.

☙

कृपया बलिं ददातु

Kṛpayā bilaṃ dadātu.

Please give me the bill.

☙

धन्यवाद:, भोजनं अतीव स्वादष्टिम् आसीत्।

Dhanyavādaḥ, bhojanaṃ atīva svādiṣṭam āsīt.

Thank you, the meal was very delicious.

൵

6. Asking for Directions

क्षम्यताम्, बसस्थानकं कुत्र अस्ति?

Kṣamyatām, basasthānakaṃ kutra asti?

Excuse me, where is the bus stop?

൵

एतत् दक्षणिदिशि अस्ति।

Etat dakṣiṇadiśi asti.

It is to the south.

❀

रेलस्थानकं कियत् दूरे अस्ति?

Relasthānakaṃ kiyat dūre asti?

How far is the railway station?

❀

अत्रतः एकं किलोमीटरम्।

Atrataḥ ekaṃ kilomīṭaram.

It is one kilometer from here.

❀

कृपया मार्गं दर्शयतु।

Kṛpayā mārgaṃ darśayatu.

Please show me the way.

৳৩

7. Health and Emergencies

अहं अस्वस्थः अस्मि।

Ahaṃ asvasthaḥ asmi.

I am unwell.

৳৩

वैद्यः कुत्र अस्ति?

Vaidyaḥ kutra asti?

Where is the doctor?

৳৩

मम शरिः पीडयतिा

Mama śiraḥ pīḍayati.

My head is hurting.

౷

कृपया औषधं ददातु।

Kṛpayā auṣadhaṃ dadātu.

Please give me medicine.

౷

अत्र आपत्कालीनसेवा किम्?

Atra āpatkālīnasevā kim?

What is the emergency service here?

౷

8. Travel and Transportation

अहं रेलयानेन गच्छामि

Ahaṃ relayānena gacchāmi.

I am going by train.

৪৩

टकिटं कुत्र प्राप्यते?

Ṭikaṭaṃ kutra prāpyate?

Where can I get a ticket?

৪৩

अग्रिमं बसः कदा आगच्छति?

Agrimaṃ basaḥ kadā āgacchati?

When does the next bus arrive?

ॐ

अहं विमानस्थानकं गच्छामि

Ahaṃ vimānasthānakaṃ gacchāmi.

I am going to the airport.

ॐ

कृपया मां स्टेशने स्थापयतु

Kṛpayā māṃ sṭeśane sthāpayatu.

Please drop me at the station.

ॐ

9. Weather and Seasons

अद्य वातावरणं कथं अस्ति?

Adya vātāvaraṇam katham asti?

How is the weather today?

౮౬

अद्य वृष्टिः भविष्यति।

Adya vṛṣṭiḥ bhaviṣyati.

It will rain today.

౮౬

ग्रीष्मकालः अतीव उष्णः अस्ति।

Grīṣmakālaḥ atīva uṣṇaḥ asti.

Summer is very hot.

౮౬

शीतकालः आगच्छति।

Śītakālaḥ āgacchati.

Winter is coming.

৳৩

वसन्तकाले प्रकृतिः सुन्दरा भवति।

Vasantakāle prakṛtiḥ sundarā bhavati.

Nature becomes beautiful in spring.

৳৩

10. Festivals and Celebrations

दीपावल्याः शुभकामनाः।

Dīpāvalyāḥ śubhakāmanāḥ.

Happy Diwali.

౭౦

अहं होलिकोत्सवं मोदतो

Ahaṃ holikotsavaṃ modate.

I enjoy the Holi festival.

౭౦

रामनवम्याः शुभकामनाः।

Rāmanavamyāḥ śubhakāmanāḥ.

Happy Ram Navami.

౭౦

अहं उत्सवे गच्छामि

Aham utsave gacchāmi.

I am going to the festival.

౭౦

उत्सवः अतीव आनन्ददायकः अस्ति

Utsavaḥ atīva ānandadāyakaḥ asti.

The festival is very joyful.

౭౦

Multiple Type Questions

   1. Greetings and Introductions
   What does "नमस्ते" (Namaste) mean?
a) Goodbye
b) Thank you
c) Hello
d) Sorry
Answer: c) Hello

• 62 •

2. How do you ask someone's name formally in Sanskrit?

a) भवतः नाम किम्?

b) त्वं कुत्र गच्छसि?

c) कः किरोति?

d) कदा आगच्छसि?

Answer: a) भवतः नाम किम्?

3. How do you say "I live in Delhi" in Sanskrit?

a) अहं विद्यालयं गच्छामि।

b) अहं दिल्लीनगरे वसामि।

c) अहं ग्रामे वसामि।

d) अहं पठामि।

Answer: b) अहं दिल्लीनगरे वसामि।

4. How do you ask "What day is today?" in Sanskrit?

a) कः किरोति?

b) अद्य कः दिवसः?

c) कदा आगच्छसि?

d) गृहे कः अस्ति?

Answer: b) अद्य कः दिवसः?

5. What is the Sanskrit word for "Monday"?

a) सोमवासरः

b) मङ्गलवासरः

c) शनिवासरः

d) शुक्रवासरः

Answer: a) सोमवासरः

6. What is the meaning of "शिक्षकः कुत्र अस्ति?"

a) Where is the teacher?

b) What is the teacher doing?

c) Where is the book?

d) Who is the teacher?

Answer: a) Where is the teacher?

7. What does "मातः, अहं क्षुधार्तः अस्मि।" mean?

a) Mother, I am thirsty.

b) Mother, I am hungry.

c) Mother, I am tired.

d) Mother, I am going out.

Answer: b) Mother, I am hungry.

8. How do you say "Brother, what are you doing?" in Sanskrit?

a) भ्रातः, त्वं किं किरोषि?

b) भगिनि, त्वं किं किरोषि?

c) मातः, त्वं किं किरोति?

d) पिता, किं किरोति?

Answer: a) भ्रातः, त्वं किं किरोषि?

9. What does "गृहे कः आगच्छति?" mean?

a) Who is coming home?

b) What is inside the house?

c) Where is the teacher?

d) Who is at the temple?

Answer: a) Who is coming home?

10. How do you ask "How much does this cost?" in Sanskrit?

a) किं किरोति?

b) इदं कियत् मूल्यम् अस्ति?

c) किं पठति?

d) कः कर्तुम् इच्छति?

Answer: b) इदं कियत् मूल्यम् अस्ति?

11. What is the Sanskrit word for "fifty rupees"?

a) दश रूप्यकाणि

b) पञ्चाशत् रूप्यकाणि

c) एक रूप्यकाणि

d) शत रूप्यकाणि

Answer: b) पञ्चाशत् रूप्यकाणि

12. What does "कृपया बिलं ददातु" mean?

a) Please give me water.

b) Please give me the bill.

c) Please give me food.

d) Please bring a chair.

Answer: b) Please give me the bill.

13. How do you say "I want to drink water" in Sanskrit?

a) अहं जलं पातुम् इच्छामि।

b) अहं भोजनं करिष्यामि।

c) अहं फलानि पातुम् इच्छामि।

d) अहं नृत्यति।

Answer: a) अहं जलं पातुम् इच्छामि।

14. What does "बसस्थानकं कुत्र अस्ति?" mean?

a) Where is the bus stop?

b) Where is the railway station?

c) Where is the house?

d) Where is the temple?

Answer: a) Where is the bus stop?

15. How do you say "Please show me the way" in Sanskrit?

a) कृपया मार्गं दर्शयतु।

b) कृपया द्रष्टुम् इच्छति।

c) कृपया समीपं आगच्छ।

d) कृपया भोजनं ददातु।

Answer: a) कृपया मार्गं दर्शयतु।

16. How do you say "I am unwell" in Sanskrit?

a) अहं अस्वस्थः अस्मि।

b) अहं स्वस्थः अस्मि।

c) अहं गच्छामि।

d) अहं पठामि।

Answer: a) अहं अस्वस्थः अस्मि।

17. What does "मम शिरः पीडयति" mean?

a) My leg is hurting.

b) My stomach is paining.

c) My head is hurting.

d) My hand is injured.

Answer: c) My head is hurting.

18. How do you ask "Where can I get a ticket?" in Sanskrit?

a) अत्र टिकिटं अस्ति?

b) टिकटं कुत्र प्राप्यते?

c) अहं टिकटं इच्छामि।

d) मार्गं दर्शयतु।

Answer: b) टिकटं कुत्र प्राप्यते?

19. What does "अहं विमानस्थानकं गच्छामि" mean?

a) I am going to the railway station.

b) I am going to the airport.

c) I am going to the school.

d) I am going to the house.

Answer: b) I am going to the airport.

20. How do you say "It will rain today" in Sanskrit?

a) अद्य वृष्टिः भविष्यति।

b) अद्य ग्रीष्मकालः अस्ति।

c) अद्य हिमं भविष्यति।

d) अद्य वायुः वेगेन वहति।

Answer: a) अद्य वृष्टिः भविष्यति।

21. What does "दीपावल्याः शुभकामनाः।" mean?

a) Happy Holi.

b) Happy Diwali.

c) Happy New Year.

d) Happy Birthday.

Answer: b) Happy Diwali.

22. How do you say "I am going to the festival" in Sanskrit?

a) अहं उत्सवे गच्छामि।

b) अहं विद्यालयं गच्छामि।

c) अहं पर्वतं गच्छामि।

d) अहं गृहे गच्छामि।

Answer: a) अहं उत्सवे गच्छामि।

23. What does "ग्रीष्मकालः अतीव उष्णः अस्ति" mean?

a) Summer is very cold.

b) Summer is very hot.

c) Winter is very warm.

d) It is raining in summer.

Answer: b) Summer is very hot.

24. How do you say "Winter is coming" in Sanskrit?

a) शीतकाल: आगच्छति।

b) वर्षा आगच्छति।

c) वसन्तकाल: अस्ति।

d) अद्य उष्णता अस्ति।

Answer: a) शीतकाल: आगच्छति।

25. What does "उत्सव: अतीव आनन्ददायक: अस्ति।" mean?

a) The festival is very joyful.
b) The festival is over.
c) The festival is boring.
d) The festival is expensive.
Answer: a) The festival is very joyful.

V

Sanskrit Proverbs and Sayings

1. अहिंसा परमो धर्मः।

Ahimsā paramo dharmaḥ.

Meaning: Non-violence is the highest duty.

Context: Emphasizes the importance of non-violence in life.

2. सत्यमेव जयते।

Satyameva jayate.

Meaning: Truth alone triumphs.

Context: A reminder that truth always prevails in the end.

3. विद्या ददाति विनयम्।

Vidyā dadāti vinayam.

Meaning: Knowledge gives humility.

Context: True education leads to humility and good behavior.

4. अतिथिदेवो भव।

Atithi devo bhava.

Meaning: Treat your guest as God.

Context: Highlights the importance of hospitality in Indian culture.

5. उद्यमेन हि सिध्यन्ति कार्याणि न मनोरथैः।

Udyamena hi sidhyanti kāryāṇi na manorathaiḥ.

Meaning: Success is achieved through hard work, not just by wishing.

Context: Encourages diligence and effort.

6. कर्मण्येवाधिकारस्ते मा फलेषु कदाचन।

Karmaṇyevādhikāraste mā phaleṣu kadācana.

Meaning: You have the right to work, but not to the fruits of work.

Context: From the Bhagavad Gita, emphasizing selfless action.

7. यत् भावो तत् भवति।

Yat bhāvo tat bhavati.

Meaning: As you think, so you become.

Context: Highlights the power of thoughts and intentions.

8. स्वस्थस्य स्वास्थ्य रक्षणम्।

Svasthasya svāsthya rakṣaṇam.

Meaning: The protection of health is the duty of the healthy.

Context: Stresses the importance of maintaining good health.

9. धर्मो रक्षति रक्षतिः।

Dharmo rakṣati rakṣitaḥ.

Meaning: Dharma protects those who protect it.

Context: Upholding righteousness ensures protection.

10. अलसस्य कुतो वद्यिा, अवद्यिस्य कुतो धनम्।

Alasasya kuto vidyā, avidyasya kuto dhanam.

Meaning: How can a lazy person gain knowledge? How can an ignorant person gain wealth?

Context: Encourages hard work and learning.

11. सर्व ंपरवश ंद:ुख,ं सर्वमात्मवश ंसुखम्।

Sarvaṃ paravaśaṃ duḥkhaṃ, sarvamātmavaśaṃ sukham.

Meaning: All that is controlled by others is sorrow; all that is self-controlled is happiness.

Context: Emphasizes self-reliance and independence.

12. वद्यिाधन ंसर्वधनप्रधानम्।

Vidyādhanaṃ sarvadhanapradhānam.

Meaning: The wealth of knowledge is the greatest wealth.

Context: Knowledge is more valuable than material possessions.

13. श्रद्धावान् लभते ज्ञानम्।

Śraddhāvān labhate jñānam.

Meaning: The devoted one attains knowledge.

Context: Faith and dedication lead to wisdom.

14. नास्ति विद्या समं चक्षुः।

Nāsti vidyā samaṃ cakṣuḥ.

Meaning: There is no eye like knowledge.

Context: Knowledge is the greatest tool for understanding the world.

15. धैर्यं साहसकिता च।

Dhairyaṃ sāhasikatā ca.

Meaning: Patience and courage.

Context: Success comes to those who are patient and brave.

16. परोपकाराय पुण्याय, पापाय परपीडनम्।

Paropakārāya puṇyāya, pāpāya parapīḍanam.

Meaning: Helping others is virtuous; harming others is sinful.

Context: Encourages kindness and compassion.

17. यथा राजा तथा प्रजा।

Yathā rājā tathā prajā.

Meaning: As the king, so are the subjects.

Context: Leaders set the tone for their followers.

18. अभ्यासेन तु कौन्तेय, वैराग्येण च गृह्यते।

Abhyāsena tu Kaunteya, vairāgyeṇa ca gṛhyate.

Meaning: Practice and detachment lead to success.

Context: From the Bhagavad Gita, emphasizing discipline and detachment.

19. न चोरहार्यं न च राजहार्यं।

Na corahāryaṃ na ca rājahāryaṃ.

Meaning: Neither can thieves steal it, nor can kings take it away.

Context: Refers to the eternal nature of knowledge.

20. सुखार्थिनः कुतो वद्यिा, वद्यिार्थिनः कुतो सुखम्।

Sukhārthinaḥ kuto vidyā, vidyārthinaḥ kuto sukham.

Meaning: Those who seek comfort cannot gain knowledge; those who seek knowledge cannot gain comfort.

Context: Learning requires sacrifice and effort.

21. गुरुर्ब्रह्मा गुरुर्वष्णिुः गुरुर्देवो महेश्वरः।

Gururbrahmā gururviṣṇuḥ gururdevo maheśvaraḥ.

Meaning: The teacher is Brahma, Vishnu, and Shiva.

Context: Highlights the importance of a teacher in one's life.

22. वसुधैव कुटुम्बकम्।

Vasudhaiva kuṭumbakam.

Meaning: The world is one family.

Context: Promotes universal brotherhood and unity.

23. अज्ञानतमिरिन्धस्य ज्ञानाञ्जनशलाकया।

Ajñānatimirāndhasya jñānāñjanaśalākayā.

Meaning: Knowledge is the light that dispels the darkness of ignorance.

Context: The power of knowledge to enlighten.

24. यद्भावो तद्भवति।

Yadbhāvo tadbhavati.

Meaning: As you think, so you become.

Context: The power of positive thinking.

25. धर्म एव हतो हन्ति धर्मो रक्षति रक्षितः।

Dharma eva hato hanti dharmo rakṣati rakṣitaḥ.

Meaning: Dharma destroys when destroyed; Dharma protects when protected.

Context: The importance of upholding righteousness.

These Sanskrit proverbs and sayings are linguistically beautiful and carry profound philosophical and moral lessons.

Multiple Type Questions

1. Ahimsā paramo dharmaḥ.
   What does "अहिंसा परमो धर्मः" mean?
a) Violence is the supreme duty
b) Peace is not important
c) Non-violence is the highest duty
d) Duty is unnecessary
Answer: c) Non-violence is the highest duty

2. Satyameva jayate.

"सत्यमेव जयते" is associated with which concept?

a) Wealth and power

b) Truth and triumph

c) War and victory

d) Peace and patience

Answer: b) Truth and triumph

3. Vidyā dadāti vinayam.

What does knowledge give according to "विद्या ददाति विनियम्"?

a) Power

b) Humility

c) Wealth

d) Fame

Answer: b) Humility

4. Atithi devo bhava.

"अतथि देवो भव" emphasizes the importance of:

a) Education

b) Hospitality

c) Friendship

d) Justice

Answer: b) Hospitality

5. Udyamena hi sidhyanti kāryāṇi na manorathaiḥ.

According to "उद्यमेन हि सिध्यन्ति कार्याणि न मनोरथैः", success is achieved by:

a) Hard work

b) Daydreaming

c) Magic

d) Luck

Answer: a) Hard work

6. Karmaṇyevādhikāraste mā phaleṣu kadācana.

The Bhagavad Gita teaches in "कर्मण्येवाधिकारस्ते मा फलेषु कदाचन" that one has the right to:

a) The results of work

b) Work itself, not the results

c) Only good deeds

d) Wealth

Answer: b) Work itself, not the results

7. Yat bhāvo tat bhavati.

"यत् भावो तत् भवति" signifies the power of:

a) Food

b) Thoughts

c) Destiny

d) Wealth

Answer: b) Thoughts

8. Svasthasya svāsthya rakṣaṇam.

"स्वस्थस्य स्वास्थ्य रक्षणम्" means that it is the duty of the healthy to:

a) Eat more

b) Protect their health

c) Visit the doctor regularly

d) Ignore fitness

Answer: b) Protect their health

9. Dharmo rakṣati rakṣitaḥ.

What does "धर्मो रक्षति रक्षति:" mean?

a) Dharma protects those who uphold it

b) Religion is unnecessary

c) Power comes from money

d) Knowledge leads to strength

Answer: a) Dharma protects those who uphold it

10. Alasasya kuto vidyā, avidyasya kuto dhanam.

What is emphasized in "अलसस्य कुतो विद्या, अविद्यस्य कुतो धनम्"?

a) Laziness leads to knowledge

b) Knowledge and wealth require effort

c) Only wealth is important

d) Ignorance is bliss

Answer: b) Knowledge and wealth require effort

11. Sarvaṃ paravaśaṃ duḥkhaṃ, sarvamātmavaśaṃ sukham.

According to "सर्व परवश दुःख, सर्वमात्मवश सुखम्", what leads to happiness?

a) Being controlled by others

b) Self-control

c) Following society

d) Ignorance

Answer: b) Self-control

12. Vidyādhanaṃ sarvadhanapradhānam.

Which wealth is the greatest according to "वद्यिाधन ंसर्वधनप्रधानम्"?

a) Gold

b) Money

c) Knowledge

d) Land

Answer: c) Knowledge

13. Śraddhāvān labhate jñānam.

What is required to attain knowledge according to "श्रद्धावान् लभत ेज्ञानम्"?

a) Wealth

b) Dedication and faith

c) Physical strength

d) Luck

Answer: b) Dedication and faith

14. Nāsti vidyā samaṃ cakṣuḥ.

"नास्ति विद्या सम ंचक्ष:ु" means:

a) Knowledge is the greatest vision

b) Knowledge is useless

c) Eyesight is more important than learning

d) Strength is greater than wisdom

Answer: a) Knowledge is the greatest vision

15. Dhairyaṃ sāhasikatā ca.

Success comes from:

a) Laziness and carelessness

b) Patience and courage

c) Money and status

d) Fear and hesitation

Answer: b) Patience and courage

16. Paropakārāya puṇyāya, pāpāya parapīḍanam.

What leads to virtue according to "परोपकाराय पुण्याय, पापाय परपीडनम्"?

a) Helping others

b) Harming others

c) Ignoring others

d) Thinking only about oneself

Answer: a) Helping others

17. Yathā rājā tathā prajā.

"यथा राजा तथा प्रजा" means:

a) The king and subjects are different

b) Leaders influence their people

c) The subjects control the king

d) The king has no role in governance

Answer: b) Leaders influence their people

18. Abhyāsena tu Kaunteya, vairāgyeṇa ca gṛhyate.

"अभ्यासेन तु कौन्तेय, वैराग्येण च गह्यते" highlights the importance of:

a) Practice and detachment

b) Strength and money

c) War and fighting

d) Blind faith

Answer: a) Practice and detachment

19. Na corahāryaṃ na ca rājahāryaṃ.

What cannot be stolen according to "न चोरहार्यं न च राजहार्य"?

a) Gold

b) Knowledge

c) Land

d) Food

Answer: b) Knowledge

20. Sukhārthinaḥ kuto vidyā, vidyārthinaḥ kuto sukham.

What is needed to gain knowledge according to "सुखार्थनिः कुतो वदिया, वदियार्थनिः कुतो सुखम्"?

a) Hard work and sacrifice

b) Enjoyment and laziness

c) Ignorance

d) Luck

Answer: a) Hard work and sacrifice

21-25 (Shortened for Brevity)

Who is considered divine in "गुरूर्ब्रह्मा गुरूर्वष्णिुः गुरूर्देवो महेश्वरः"? (Answer: Teacher)

What does "वसुधैव कटुम्बकम्" mean? (Answer: The world is one family)

What removes ignorance in "अज्ञानतमिरिान्धस्य ज्ञानाञ्जनशलाकया"? (Answer: Knowledge)

"यद्भावो तद्भवति" teaches us about? (Answer: Power of thoughts)

"धर्म एव हतो हन्ति धर्मो रक्षति रक्षति:" emphasizes? (Answer: Dharma must be protected)

VI
Sanskrit in Daily Life

Sanskrit, often regarded as the "language of the gods," is an ancient language and a living part of daily life in many ways. While it is no longer widely spoken as a first language, its *influence permeates various aspects of modern life, especially in India.*

Here's how Sanskrit is still relevant in daily life:

1. Religious and Spiritual Practices

Chants and Mantras: Sanskrit is the language of most Hindu prayers, chants, and mantras. For example:

गायत्री मन्त्र: (Gāyatrī Mantra): A powerful Vedic chant for wisdom.

ॐ (Om): The universal sound used in meditation and yoga.

Rituals and Ceremonies: Sanskrit is used in weddings, funerals, and other rituals.

Temple Prayers: Many temple hymns and prayers are in Sanskrit.

2. Yoga and Meditation

Yoga Terms: Sanskrit is the language of yoga. Common terms include:

आसन (Āsana): Yoga posture.

पृराणायाम *(Prāṇāyāma): Breath control.*

ध्यान *(Dhyāna): Meditation.*

Chanting: Many yoga classes begin or end with Sanskrit chants like लोका: समस्ता: सुखिनो भवन्तु *(Lokāḥ Samastāḥ Sukhino Bhavantu) – "May all beings be happy."*

3. Festivals and Celebrations

Festival Greetings: Sanskrit phrases are used during festivals:

दीपावल्या: शुभकामना: *(Dīpāvalyāḥ Śubhakāmanāḥ): Happy Diwali.*

नववर्षस्य शुभकामना: *(Navavarṣasya Śubhakāmanāḥ): Happy New Year.*

Rituals: Many festival rituals involve Sanskrit mantras and hymns.

4. Education and Learning

School Curriculum: Sanskrit is taught in schools across India as a second or third language.

Scholarship: Sanskrit is studied for its rich literature, including the Vedas, Upanishads, and epics like the Ramayana and Mahabharata.

Sanskrit Universities: Institutions like Sampurnanand Sanskrit University and Rashtriya Sanskrit Sansthan promote Sanskrit learning.

5. Names and Naming Conventions

Personal Names: Many Indian names are derived from Sanskrit, such as:

अर्जुन *(Arjuna): A hero from the Mahabharata.*

सीता *(Sītā): The wife of Lord Rama.*

Place Names: Cities like हरद्विार *(Haridwār) and* वाराणसी *(Vārāṇasī) have Sanskrit origins.*

6. Literature and Arts

Classical Texts: Sanskrit literature includes timeless works like:

रामायणम् *(Rāmāyaṇam): The epic of Rama.*

महाभारतम् *(Mahābhāratam): The epic of the Kuru dynasty.*

भगवद्गीता *(Bhagavadgītā): A spiritual discourse from the Mahabharata.*

Drama and Poetry: Sanskrit plays like अभिज्ञानशाकुन्तलम् (Abhijñānaśākuntalam) by Kalidasa are still performed.

7. Science and Mathematics

Ancient Contributions: Sanskrit texts contain advanced knowledge in:

Astronomy: Texts like सूर्य सिद्धान्त (Sūrya Siddhānta).

Mathematics: Concepts like zero and the decimal system originated in Sanskrit texts.

Medicine: आयुर्वेद (Āyurveda) is based on Sanskrit texts like चरक संहिता (Caraka Saṃhitā).

8. Modern Media and Technology

Films and Music: Sanskrit is used in movies, songs, and documentaries. For example, the song "Deva Shree Ganesha" from the movie Agneepath includes Sanskrit verses.

Digital Tools: Apps and websites now offer Sanskrit learning resources, translations, and dictionaries.

Social Media: Sanskrit is gaining popularity on platforms like Twitter and YouTube, with hashtags like #SanskritRevival.

9. Government and Official Use

Mottos and Slogans: Many Indian institutions use Sanskrit mottos:

सत्यमेव जयते *(Satyameva Jayate): "Truth alone triumphs" (National Emblem of India).*

योग: कर्मसु कौशलम् *(Yogaḥ Karmasu Kauśalam): "Yoga is skill in action" (Motto of the Indian Army).*

Coins and Stamps: Sanskrit phrases are often inscribed on Indian currency and stamps.

10. Everyday Phrases and Expressions

Common Greetings:

नमस्ते *(Namaste): Hello.*

धन्यवाद: *(Dhanyavādaḥ): Thank you.*

स्वागतम् *(Svāgatam): Welcome.*

Proverbs and Sayings: Sanskrit proverbs like अहिंसा परमो धर्म: *(Ahimsā Paramo Dharmaḥ) – "Non-violence is the highest duty" – are widely quoted.*

11. Cultural Identity

National Pride: Sanskrit symbolises India's ancient heritage and cultural identity.

Revival Efforts: Organizations and individuals are working to revive Sanskrit as a spoken language through workshops, camps, and online courses.

12. Global Influence

Yoga and Meditation: Sanskrit terms like कर्म *(Karma) and* मोक्ष *(Mokṣa) are recognized worldwide.*

Academic Interest: Universities globally offer courses in Sanskrit for its linguistic, literary, and philosophical value.

Examples of Sanskrit in Daily Life

Morning Rituals: Chanting गायत्री मन्त्र: *(Gāyatrī Mantra) during prayers.*

Yoga Class: Practicing सूर्य नमस्कार *(Sūrya Namaskār) – Sun Salutation.*

Festivals: Reciting श्लोकाः (Ślokāḥ) during Diwali or Navaratri.

Education: Learning Sanskrit shlokas in school.

Names: Naming a child अनन्या (Ananyā) – "Unique" or आदित्य (Āditya) – "Sun."

Sanskrit is not just a language of the past; it is a living tradition that inspires and guides millions daily.

Multiple Type Questions

1. Which of the following Sanskrit phrases means "Truth alone triumphs"?

a) वसुधैव कुटुम्बकम्

b) सत्यमेव जयते

c) कर्मण्येवाधिकारस्ते

d) अहिंसा परमो धर्मः

 Answer: (b) सत्यमेव जयते

 2. Which Sanskrit term is commonly used in yoga to refer to "breath control"?

a) आसन (Āsana)

b) प्राणायाम (Prāṇāyāma)

c) ध्यान (Dhyāna)

d) मन्त्र (Mantra)

 Answer: (b) प्राणायाम (Prāṇāyāma)

 3. Which of these Sanskrit mantras is known as a powerful Vedic chant for wisdom?

a) ॐ नमः शिवाय (Om Namaḥ Śivāya)

b) गायत्री मन्त्रः (Gāyatrī Mantra)

c) महा मृत्युञ्जय मन्त्र (Mahā Mṛtyuñjaya Mantra)

d) हनुमान चालीसा (Hanumān Chālīsā)

 Answer: (b) गायत्री मन्त्रः (Gāyatrī Mantra)

4. Which of the following Sanskrit phrases is used to wish someone "Happy Diwali"?

a) दीपावल्या: शुभकामना:

b) नववर्षस्य शुभकामना:

c) जन्मदिनस्य शुभाशया:

d) वसुधैव कुटुम्बकम्

Answer: (a) दीपावल्या: शुभकामना:

5. The phrase "अहिंसा परमो धर्म:" signifies the importance of:

a) Truth

b) Non-violence

c) Hospitality

d) Knowledge

Answer: (b) Non-violence

6. The Bhagavad Gita was originally written in which language?

a) Hindi

b) Pali

c) Sanskrit

d) Tamil

Answer: (c) Sanskrit

7. Which of the following terms is related to Ayurveda?

a) चरक संहिता (Caraka Saṃhitā)

b) महाभारतम् (Mahābhāratam)

c) रामायणम् (Rāmāyaṇam)

d) गीतगोविन्दम् (Gīta Govindam)

Answer: (a) चरक संहिता (Caraka Saṃhitā)

8. Which of these Sanskrit phrases means "The world is one family"?

a) सर्वं परवश दुःखं

b) वसुधैव कुटुम्बकम्

c) श्रद्धावान् लभते ज्ञानम्

d) नास्ति विद्या समं चक्षु:

Answer: (b) वसुधैव कुटुम्बकम्

9. The phrase "विद्या ददाति विनयम्" highlights the importance of:

a) Wealth

b) Education

c) Humility

d) Hard work

Answer: (c) Humility

10. Which of the following is NOT a Sanskrit name?

a) अर्जुन (Arjuna)

b) सीता (Sītā)

c) हरद्विार (Haridwār)

d) लंदन (London)

Answer: (d) लंदन (London)

11. Which Sanskrit epic narrates the story of Lord Rama?

a) महाभारतम्

b) भागवतम्

c) रामायणम्

d) अर्थशास्त्र

Answer: (c) रामायणम्

12. What does the Sanskrit term "स्वागतम्" mean?

a) Welcome

b) Goodbye

c) Thank You

d) Sorry

Answer: (a) Welcome

13. Which Sanskrit text is associated with astronomy?

a) सूर्य सद्धिान्त (Sūrya Siddhānta)

b) अभज्ञिानशाकुन्तलम् (Abhijñānaśākuntalam)

c) पंचतंत्र (Pañcatantra)

d) योगसूत्र (Yoga Sūtra)

Answer: (a) सूर्य सद्धिान्त (Sūrya Siddhānta)

14. The phrase "कर्मण्येवाधिकारस्ते मा फलेषु कदाचन" is from which sacred text?

a) रामायण

b) महाभारत

c) भगवद्गीता

d) योगसूत्र

Answer: (c) भगवद्गीता

15. Which of these is a famous Sanskrit drama written by Kalidasa?

a) गीतगोविन्दम्

b) पंचतंत्र

c) अभिज्ञानशाकुन्तलम्

d) अर्थशास्त्र

Answer: (c) अभिज्ञानशाकुन्तलम्

16. What is the Sanskrit equivalent of "Thank you"?

a) नमस्ते

b) धन्यवाद:

c) स्वागतम्

d) शांति

Answer: (b) धन्यवाद:

17. Which Sanskrit phrase is commonly used in meditation?

a) ॐ (Om)

b) नम: शिवाय (Namaḥ Śivāya)

c) हरि ॐ (Hari Om)

d) All of the above

Answer: (d) All of the above

18. Which ancient Indian scripture primarily discusses health and medicine?

a) योगसूत्र (Yoga Sūtra)

b) आयुर्वेद (Āyurveda)

c) गीता (Gītā)

d) महाभारत (Mahābhārata)

Answer: (b) आयुर्वेद (Āyurveda)

19. What does "नास्ति विद्या सम चक्षु:" mean?

a) Knowledge is the best vision

b) Hard work leads to success

c) Dharma protects those who protect it

d) Knowledge gives humility

Answer: (a) Knowledge is the best vision

20. Which Sanskrit phrase means "Helping others is a virtue"?

a) परोपकाराय पुण्याय

b) अहिंसा परमो धर्मः

c) यथा राजा तथा प्रजा

d) कर्मण्येवाधिकि Answer: (a) परोपकाराय पुण्याय

21. Which university promotes Sanskrit learning in India?

a) IIT Delhi

b) Jawaharlal Nehru University

c) Sampurnanand Sanskrit University

d) Banaras Hindu University

Answer: (c) Sampurnanand Sanskrit University

22. Which Indian currency symbol is derived from Sanskrit?

a)   ₹ (Rupee)

b) $ (Dollar)

c) € (Euro)

d) £ (Pound)

Answer: (a)   ₹ (Rupee)

23. Which phrase means "Patience and Courage"?

a) धैर्यं साहसकिता च

b) सत्यमेव जयते

c) श्रद्धावान् लभते ज्ञानम्

d) नास्ति विद्या समं चक्षुः

Answer: (a) धैर्यं साहसकिता च

24. Which Sanskrit phrase is India's national motto?

Answer: सत्यमेव जयते

25. What is the meaning of "लोकाः समस्ताः सुखिनो भवन्तु"?

Answer: May all beings be happy.

BOOKS BY THE SAME AUTHOR

Scan Here
FOR QUALITY BOOKS
For Home Library for
Parents, Educators &Students